Vehicle

Maintenance Log

for Dad

Motor Vehicle Particulars

Make: _____

Model: _____

Year: _____

Chassis # _____

Engine No.: _____

Year Purchased: _____

Service Providers

Name:	
Contact No.:	
Address:	

Name:	
Contact No.:	
Address:	

Name:	
Contact No.:	
Address:	

Name:	
Contact No.:	
Address:	

Name:	
Contact No.:	
Address:	

Name:	
Contact No.:	
Address:	

Name:	
Contact No.:	
Address:	

Service Record Sheet

Service Date:	Mileage at Service:
Service Provider:	Cost:

Scope of Work: _____
_____
_____

Review/Notes: _____
_____
_____

Service Date:	Mileage at Service:
Service Provider:	Cost:

Scope of Work: _____
_____
_____

Review/Notes: _____
_____
_____

Service Date:	Mileage at Service:
Service Provider:	Cost:

Scope of Work: _____
_____
_____

Review/Notes: _____
_____
_____

Service Record Sheet

Service Date:	Mileage at Service:
Service Provider:	Cost:

Scope of Work: _____
_____
_____
_____

Review/Notes: _____
_____
_____

Service Date:	Mileage at Service:
Service Provider:	Cost:

Scope of Work: _____
_____
_____
_____

Review/Notes: _____
_____
_____

Service Date:	Mileage at Service:
Service Provider:	Cost:

Scope of Work: _____
_____
_____
_____

Review/Notes: _____
_____
_____

Service Record Sheet

Service Date:	Mileage at Service:
Service Provider:	Cost:

Scope of Work: _____
_____
_____

Review/Notes: _____
_____
_____

Service Date:	Mileage at Service:
Service Provider:	Cost:

Scope of Work: _____
_____
_____

Review/Notes: _____
_____
_____

Service Date:	Mileage at Service:
Service Provider:	Cost:

Scope of Work: _____
_____
_____

Review/Notes: _____
_____
_____

Service Record Sheet

Service Date:	Mileage at Service:
Service Provider:	Cost:

Scope of Work: _____
_____
_____

Review/Notes: _____
_____
_____

Service Date:	Mileage at Service:
Service Provider:	Cost:

Scope of Work: _____
_____
_____

Review/Notes: _____
_____
_____

Service Date:	Mileage at Service:
Service Provider:	Cost:

Scope of Work: _____
_____
_____

Review/Notes: _____
_____
_____

Service Record Sheet

Service Date:	Mileage at Service:
Service Provider:	Cost:

Scope of Work: _____
_____
_____

Review/Notes: _____
_____
_____

Service Date:	Mileage at Service:
Service Provider:	Cost:

Scope of Work: _____
_____
_____

Review/Notes: _____
_____
_____

Service Date:	Mileage at Service:
Service Provider:	Cost:

Scope of Work: _____
_____
_____

Review/Notes: _____
_____
_____

Service Record Sheet

Service Date:	Mileage at Service:
Service Provider:	Cost:

Scope of Work: _____

_____

_____

Review/Notes: _____

_____

_____

Service Date:	Mileage at Service:
Service Provider:	Cost:

Scope of Work: _____

_____

_____

Review/Notes: _____

_____

_____

Service Date:	Mileage at Service:
Service Provider:	Cost:

Scope of Work: _____

_____

_____

Review/Notes: _____

_____

_____

Service Record Sheet

Service Date:	Mileage at Service:
Service Provider:	Cost:

Scope of Work: _____
_____
_____

Review/Notes: _____
_____
_____

Service Date:	Mileage at Service:
Service Provider:	Cost:

Scope of Work: _____
_____
_____

Review/Notes: _____
_____
_____

Service Date:	Mileage at Service:
Service Provider:	Cost:

Scope of Work: _____
_____
_____

Review/Notes: _____
_____
_____

Service Record Sheet

Service Date:	Mileage at Service:
Service Provider:	Cost:

Scope of Work: _____
_____
_____

Review/Notes: _____
_____
_____

Service Date:	Mileage at Service:
Service Provider:	Cost:

Scope of Work: _____
_____
_____

Review/Notes: _____
_____
_____

Service Date:	Mileage at Service:
Service Provider:	Cost:

Scope of Work: _____
_____
_____

Review/Notes: _____
_____
_____

Service Record Sheet

Service Date:	Mileage at Service:
Service Provider:	Cost:

Scope of Work: _____
_____
_____

Review/Notes: _____
_____
_____

Service Date:	Mileage at Service:
Service Provider:	Cost:

Scope of Work: _____
_____
_____

Review/Notes: _____
_____
_____

Service Date:	Mileage at Service:
Service Provider:	Cost:

Scope of Work: _____
_____
_____

Review/Notes: _____
_____
_____

Service Record Sheet

Service Date:	Mileage at Service:
Service Provider:	Cost:

Scope of Work: _____

_____

_____

Review/Notes: _____

_____

_____

Service Date:	Mileage at Service:
Service Provider:	Cost:

Scope of Work: _____

_____

_____

Review/Notes: _____

_____

_____

Service Date:	Mileage at Service:
Service Provider:	Cost:

Scope of Work: _____

_____

_____

Review/Notes: _____

_____

_____

Service Record Sheet

Service Date:	Mileage at Service:
Service Provider:	Cost:

Scope of Work: _____
_____
_____

Review/Notes: _____
_____
_____

Service Date:	Mileage at Service:
Service Provider:	Cost:

Scope of Work: _____
_____
_____

Review/Notes: _____
_____
_____

Service Date:	Mileage at Service:
Service Provider:	Cost:

Scope of Work: _____
_____
_____

Review/Notes: _____
_____
_____

Service Record Sheet

Service Date:	Mileage at Service:
Service Provider:	Cost:

Scope of Work: _____

_____

_____

Review/Notes: _____

_____

_____

Service Date:	Mileage at Service:
Service Provider:	Cost:

Scope of Work: _____

_____

_____

Review/Notes: _____

_____

_____

Service Date:	Mileage at Service:
Service Provider:	Cost:

Scope of Work: _____

_____

_____

Review/Notes: _____

_____

_____

Service Record Sheet

Service Date:	Mileage at Service:
Service Provider:	Cost:

Scope of Work: _____
_____
_____

Review/Notes: _____
_____
_____

Service Date:	Mileage at Service:
Service Provider:	Cost:

Scope of Work: _____
_____
_____

Review/Notes: _____
_____
_____

Service Date:	Mileage at Service:
Service Provider:	Cost:

Scope of Work: _____
_____
_____

Review/Notes: _____
_____
_____

Service Record Sheet

Service Date:	Mileage at Service:
Service Provider:	Cost:

Scope of Work: _____
_____
_____

Review/Notes: _____
_____
_____

Service Date:	Mileage at Service:
Service Provider:	Cost:

Scope of Work: _____
_____
_____

Review/Notes: _____
_____
_____

Service Date:	Mileage at Service:
Service Provider:	Cost:

Scope of Work: _____
_____
_____

Review/Notes: _____
_____
_____

Service Record Sheet

Service Date:	Mileage at Service:
Service Provider:	Cost:

Scope of Work: _____
_____
_____

Review/Notes: _____
_____
_____

Service Date:	Mileage at Service:
Service Provider:	Cost:

Scope of Work: _____
_____
_____

Review/Notes: _____
_____
_____

Service Date:	Mileage at Service:
Service Provider:	Cost:

Scope of Work: _____
_____
_____

Review/Notes: _____
_____
_____

Service Record Sheet

Service Date:	Mileage at Service:
Service Provider:	Cost:

Scope of Work: _____
_____
_____

Review/Notes: _____
_____
_____

Service Date:	Mileage at Service:
Service Provider:	Cost:

Scope of Work: _____
_____
_____

Review/Notes: _____
_____
_____

Service Date:	Mileage at Service:
Service Provider:	Cost:

Scope of Work: _____
_____
_____

Review/Notes: _____
_____
_____

Service Record Sheet

Service Date:	Mileage at Service:
Service Provider:	Cost:
Scope of Work: _____	
_____	
_____	
Review/Notes: _____	
_____	
_____	

Service Date:	Mileage at Service:
Service Provider:	Cost:
Scope of Work: _____	
_____	
_____	
Review/Notes: _____	
_____	
_____	

Service Date:	Mileage at Service:
Service Provider:	Cost:
Scope of Work: _____	
_____	
_____	
Review/Notes: _____	
_____	
_____	

Service Record Sheet

Service Date:	Mileage at Service:
Service Provider:	Cost:

Scope of Work: _____

_____

_____

Review/Notes: _____

_____

_____

Service Date:	Mileage at Service:
Service Provider:	Cost:

Scope of Work: _____

_____

_____

Review/Notes: _____

_____

_____

Service Date:	Mileage at Service:
Service Provider:	Cost:

Scope of Work: _____

_____

_____

Review/Notes: _____

_____

_____

Service Record Sheet

Service Date:	Mileage at Service:
Service Provider:	Cost:

Scope of Work: _____
_____
_____

Review/Notes: _____
_____
_____

Service Date:	Mileage at Service:
Service Provider:	Cost:

Scope of Work: _____
_____
_____

Review/Notes: _____
_____
_____

Service Date:	Mileage at Service:
Service Provider:	Cost:

Scope of Work: _____
_____
_____

Review/Notes: _____
_____
_____

Service Record Sheet

Service Date:	Mileage at Service:
Service Provider:	Cost:

Scope of Work: _____
_____
_____

Review/Notes: _____
_____
_____

Service Date:	Mileage at Service:
Service Provider:	Cost:

Scope of Work: _____
_____
_____

Review/Notes: _____
_____
_____

Service Date:	Mileage at Service:
Service Provider:	Cost:

Scope of Work: _____
_____
_____

Review/Notes: _____
_____
_____

Service Record Sheet

Service Date:	Mileage at Service:
Service Provider:	Cost:

Scope of Work: _____
_____
_____

Review/Notes: _____
_____
_____

Service Date:	Mileage at Service:
Service Provider:	Cost:

Scope of Work: _____
_____
_____

Review/Notes: _____
_____
_____

Service Date:	Mileage at Service:
Service Provider:	Cost:

Scope of Work: _____
_____
_____

Review/Notes: _____
_____
_____

Service Record Sheet

Service Date:	Mileage at Service:
Service Provider:	Cost:

Scope of Work: _____
_____
_____

Review/Notes: _____
_____
_____

Service Date:	Mileage at Service:
Service Provider:	Cost:

Scope of Work: _____
_____
_____

Review/Notes: _____
_____
_____

Service Date:	Mileage at Service:
Service Provider:	Cost:

Scope of Work: _____
_____
_____

Review/Notes: _____
_____
_____

Service Record Sheet

Service Date:	Mileage at Service:
Service Provider:	Cost:

Scope of Work: _____
_____
_____

Review/Notes: _____
_____
_____

Service Date:	Mileage at Service:
Service Provider:	Cost:

Scope of Work: _____
_____
_____

Review/Notes: _____
_____
_____

Service Date:	Mileage at Service:
Service Provider:	Cost:

Scope of Work: _____
_____
_____

Review/Notes: _____
_____
_____

Service Record Sheet

Service Date:	Mileage at Service:
Service Provider:	Cost:

Scope of Work: _____
_____
_____

Review/Notes: _____
_____
_____

Service Date:	Mileage at Service:
Service Provider:	Cost:

Scope of Work: _____
_____
_____

Review/Notes: _____
_____
_____

Service Date:	Mileage at Service:
Service Provider:	Cost:

Scope of Work: _____
_____
_____

Review/Notes: _____
_____
_____

Service Record Sheet

Service Date:	Mileage at Service:
Service Provider:	Cost:

Scope of Work: _____

_____

_____

Review/Notes: _____

_____

_____

Service Date:	Mileage at Service:
Service Provider:	Cost:

Scope of Work: _____

_____

_____

Review/Notes: _____

_____

_____

Service Date:	Mileage at Service:
Service Provider:	Cost:

Scope of Work: _____

_____

_____

Review/Notes: _____

_____

_____

Service Record Sheet

Service Date:	Mileage at Service:
Service Provider:	Cost:

Scope of Work: _____

_____

_____

Review/Notes: _____

_____

_____

Service Date:	Mileage at Service:
Service Provider:	Cost:

Scope of Work: _____

_____

_____

Review/Notes: _____

_____

_____

Service Date:	Mileage at Service:
Service Provider:	Cost:

Scope of Work: _____

_____

_____

Revlew/Notes: _____

_____

_____

Service Record Sheet

Service Date:	Mileage at Service:
Service Provider:	Cost:

Scope of Work: _____
_____
_____

Review/Notes: _____
_____
_____

Service Date:	Mileage at Service:
Service Provider:	Cost:

Scope of Work: _____
_____
_____

Review/Notes: _____
_____
_____

Service Date:	Mileage at Service:
Service Provider:	Cost:

Scope of Work: _____
_____
_____

Review/Notes: _____
_____
_____

Service Record Sheet

Service Date:	Mileage at Service:
Service Provider:	Cost:

Scope of Work: _____
_____
_____

Review/Notes: _____
_____
_____

Service Date:	Mileage at Service:
Service Provider:	Cost:

Scope of Work: _____
_____
_____

Review/Notes: _____
_____
_____

Service Date:	Mileage at Service:
Service Provider:	Cost:

Scope of Work: _____
_____
_____

Review/Notes: _____
_____
_____

Service Record Sheet

Service Date:	Mileage at Service:
Service Provider:	Cost:

Scope of Work: _____

_____

_____

Review/Notes: _____

_____

_____

Service Date:	Mileage at Service:
Service Provider:	Cost:

Scope of Work: _____

_____

_____

Review/Notes: _____

_____

_____

Service Date:	Mileage at Service:
Service Provider:	Cost:

Scope of Work: _____

_____

_____

Review/Notes: _____

_____

_____

Service Record Sheet

Service Date:	Mileage at Service:
Service Provider:	Cost:

Scope of Work: _____
_____
_____

Review/Notes: _____
_____
_____

Service Date:	Mileage at Service:
Service Provider:	Cost:

Scope of Work: _____
_____
_____

Review/Notes: _____
_____
_____

Service Date:	Mileage at Service:
Service Provider:	Cost:

Scope of Work: _____
_____
_____

Review/Notes: _____
_____
_____

Service Record Sheet

Service Date:	Mileage at Service:
Service Provider:	Cost:

Scope of Work: _____
_____
_____

Review/Notes: _____
_____
_____

Service Date:	Mileage at Service:
Service Provider:	Cost:

Scope of Work: _____
_____
_____

Review/Notes: _____
_____
_____

Service Date:	Mileage at Service:
Service Provider:	Cost:

Scope of Work: _____
_____
_____

Review/Notes: _____
_____
_____

Service Record Sheet

Service Date:	Mileage at Service:
Service Provider:	Cost:

Scope of Work: _____
_____
_____

Review/Notes: _____
_____
_____

Service Date:	Mileage at Service:
Service Provider:	Cost:

Scope of Work: _____
_____
_____

Review/Notes: _____
_____
_____

Service Date:	Mileage at Service:
Service Provider:	Cost:

Scope of Work: _____
_____
_____

Review/Notes: _____
_____
_____

Service Record Sheet

Service Date:	Mileage at Service:
Service Provider:	Cost:

Scope of Work: _____
_____
_____

Review/Notes: _____
_____
_____

Service Date:	Mileage at Service:
Service Provider:	Cost:

Scope of Work: _____
_____
_____

Review/Notes: _____
_____
_____

Service Date:	Mileage at Service:
Service Provider:	Cost:

Scope of Work: _____
_____
_____

Review/Notes: _____
_____
_____

Service Record Sheet

Service Date:	Mileage at Service:
Service Provider:	Cost:

Scope of Work: _____
_____
_____

Review/Notes: _____
_____
_____

Service Date:	Mileage at Service:
Service Provider:	Cost:

Scope of Work: _____
_____
_____

Review/Notes: _____
_____
_____

Service Date:	Mileage at Service:
Service Provider:	Cost:

Scope of Work: _____
_____
_____

Review/Notes: _____
_____
_____

Service Record Sheet

Service Date:	Mileage at Service:
Service Provider:	Cost:

Scope of Work: _____

_____

_____

Review/Notes: _____

_____

_____

Service Date:	Mileage at Service:
Service Provider:	Cost:

Scope of Work: _____

_____

_____

Review/Notes: _____

_____

_____

Service Date:	Mileage at Service:
Service Provider:	Cost:

Scope of Work: _____

_____

_____

Review/Notes: _____

_____

_____

Service Record Sheet

Service Date:	Mileage at Service:
Service Provider:	Cost:

Scope of Work: _____

_____

_____

Review/Notes: _____

_____

_____

Service Date:	Mileage at Service:
Service Provider:	Cost:

Scope of Work: _____

_____

_____

Review/Notes: _____

_____

_____

Service Date:	Mileage at Service:
Service Provider:	Cost:

Scope of Work: _____

_____

_____

Review/Notes: _____

_____

_____

Service Record Sheet

Service Date:	Mileage at Service:
Service Provider:	Cost:

Scope of Work: _____
_____
_____

Review/Notes: _____
_____
_____

Service Date:	Mileage at Service:
Service Provider:	Cost:

Scope of Work: _____
_____
_____

Review/Notes: _____
_____
_____

Service Date:	Mileage at Service:
Service Provider:	Cost:

Scope of Work: _____
_____
_____

Review/Notes: _____
_____
_____

Service Record Sheet

Service Date:	Mileage at Service:
Service Provider:	Cost:

Scope of Work: _____
_____
_____

Review/Notes: _____
_____
_____

Service Date:	Mileage at Service:
Service Provider:	Cost:

Scope of Work: _____
_____
_____

Review/Notes: _____
_____
_____

Service Date:	Mileage at Service:
Service Provider:	Cost:

Scope of Work: _____
_____
_____

Review/Notes: _____
_____
_____

Service Record Sheet

Service Date:	Mileage at Service:
Service Provider:	Cost:

Scope of Work: _____
_____
_____

Review/Notes: _____
_____
_____

Service Date:	Mileage at Service:
Service Provider:	Cost:

Scope of Work: _____
_____
_____

Review/Notes: _____
_____
_____

Service Date:	Mileage at Service:
Service Provider:	Cost:

Scope of Work: _____
_____
_____

Review/Notes: _____
_____
_____

Service Record Sheet

Service Date:	Mileage at Service:
Service Provider:	Cost:
Scope of Work: _____ _____ _____	
Review/Notes: _____ _____ _____	

Service Date:	Mileage at Service:
Service Provider:	Cost:
Scope of Work: _____ _____ _____	
Review/Notes: _____ _____ _____	

Service Date:	Mileage at Service:
Service Provider:	Cost:
Scope of Work: _____ _____ _____	
Review/Notes: _____ _____ _____	

Service Record Sheet

Service Date:	Mileage at Service:
Service Provider:	Cost:

Scope of Work: _____

_____

_____

Review/Notes: _____

_____

_____

Service Date:	Mileage at Service:
Service Provider:	Cost:

Scope of Work: _____

_____

_____

Review/Notes: _____

_____

_____

Service Date:	Mileage at Service:
Service Provider:	Cost:

Scope of Work: _____

_____

_____

Review/Notes: _____

_____

_____

Service Record Sheet

Service Date:	Mileage at Service:
Service Provider:	Cost:

Scope of Work: _____

_____

_____

Review/Notes: _____

_____

_____

Service Date:	Mileage at Service:
Service Provider:	Cost:

Scope of Work: _____

_____

_____

Review/Notes: _____

_____

_____

Service Date:	Mileage at Service:
Service Provider:	Cost:

Scope of Work: _____

_____

_____

Review/Notes: _____

_____

_____

Service Record Sheet

Service Date:	Mileage at Service:
Service Provider:	Cost:

Scope of Work: _____

_____

_____

Review/Notes: _____

_____

_____

Service Date:	Mileage at Service:
Service Provider:	Cost:

Scope of Work: _____

_____

_____

Review/Notes: _____

_____

_____

Service Date:	Mileage at Service:
Service Provider:	Cost:

Scope of Work: _____

_____

_____

Review/Notes: _____

_____

_____

Service Record Sheet

Service Date:	Mileage at Service:
Service Provider:	Cost:

Scope of Work: _____
_____
_____

Review/Notes: _____
_____
_____

Service Date:	Mileage at Service:
Service Provider:	Cost:

Scope of Work: _____
_____
_____

Review/Notes: _____
_____
_____

Service Date:	Mileage at Service:
Service Provider:	Cost:

Scope of Work: _____
_____
_____

Review/Notes: _____
_____
_____

Service Record Sheet

Service Date:	Mileage at Service:
Service Provider:	Cost:

Scope of Work: _____
_____
_____

Review/Notes: _____
_____
_____

Service Date:	Mileage at Service:
Service Provider:	Cost:

Scope of Work: _____
_____
_____

Review/Notes: _____
_____
_____

Service Date:	Mileage at Service:
Service Provider:	Cost:

Scope of Work: _____
_____
_____

Review/Notes: _____
_____
_____

Service Record Sheet

Service Date:	Mileage at Service:
Service Provider:	Cost:

Scope of Work: _____
_____
_____

Review/Notes: _____
_____
_____

Service Date:	Mileage at Service:
Service Provider:	Cost:

Scope of Work: _____
_____
_____

Review/Notes: _____
_____
_____

Service Date:	Mileage at Service:
Service Provider:	Cost:

Scope of Work: _____
_____
_____

Review/Notes: _____
_____
_____

Service Record Sheet

Service Date:	Mileage at Service:
Service Provider:	Cost:

Scope of Work: _____

_____

_____

Review/Notes: _____

_____

_____

Service Date:	Mileage at Service:
Service Provider:	Cost:

Scope of Work: _____

_____

_____

Review/Notes: _____

_____

_____

Service Date:	Mileage at Service:
Service Provider:	Cost:

Scope of Work: _____

_____

_____

Review/Notes: _____

_____

_____

Service Record Sheet

Service Date:	Mileage at Service:
Service Provider:	Cost:

Scope of Work: _____
_____
_____

Review/Notes: _____
_____
_____

Service Date:	Mileage at Service:
Service Provider:	Cost:

Scope of Work: _____
_____
_____

Review/Notes: _____
_____
_____

Service Date:	Mileage at Service:
Service Provider:	Cost:

Scope of Work: _____
_____
_____

Review/Notes: _____
_____
_____

Service Record Sheet

Service Date:	Mileage at Service:
Service Provider:	Cost:

Scope of Work: _____

_____

_____

Review/Notes: _____

_____

_____

Service Date:	Mileage at Service:
Service Provider:	Cost:

Scope of Work: _____

_____

_____

Review/Notes: _____

_____

_____

Service Date:	Mileage at Service:
Service Provider:	Cost:

Scope of Work: _____

_____

_____

Review/Notes: _____

_____

_____

Service Record Sheet

Service Date:	Mileage at Service:
Service Provider:	Cost:

Scope of Work: _____

_____

_____

Review/Notes: _____

_____

_____

Service Date:	Mileage at Service:
Service Provider:	Cost:

Scope of Work: _____

_____

_____

Review/Notes: _____

_____

_____

Service Date:	Mileage at Service:
Service Provider:	Cost:

Scope of Work: _____

_____

_____

Review/Notes: _____

_____

_____

Service Record Sheet

Service Date:	Mileage at Service:
Service Provider:	Cost:

Scope of Work: _____
_____
_____

Review/Notes: _____
_____
_____

Service Date:	Mileage at Service:
Service Provider:	Cost:

Scope of Work: _____
_____
_____

Review/Notes: _____
_____
_____

Service Date:	Mileage at Service:
Service Provider:	Cost:

Scope of Work: _____
_____
_____

Review/Notes: _____
_____
_____

Service Record Sheet

Service Date:	Mileage at Service:
Service Provider:	Cost:

Scope of Work: _____
_____
_____

Review/Notes: _____
_____
_____

Service Date:	Mileage at Service:
Service Provider:	Cost:

Scope of Work: _____
_____
_____

Review/Notes: _____
_____
_____

Service Date:	Mileage at Service:
Service Provider:	Cost:

Scope of Work: _____
_____
_____

Review/Notes: _____
_____
_____

Service Record Sheet

Service Date:	Mileage at Service:
Service Provider:	Cost:

Scope of Work: _____
_____
_____

Review/Notes: _____
_____
_____

Service Date:	Mileage at Service:
Service Provider:	Cost:

Scope of Work: _____
_____
_____

Review/Notes: _____
_____
_____

Service Date:	Mileage at Service:
Service Provider:	Cost:

Scope of Work: _____
_____
_____

Review/Notes: _____
_____
_____

Service Record Sheet

Service Date:	Mileage at Service:
Service Provider:	Cost:

Scope of Work: _____
_____
_____

Review/Notes: _____
_____
_____

Service Date:	Mileage at Service:
Service Provider:	Cost:

Scope of Work: _____
_____
_____

Review/Notes: _____
_____
_____

Service Date:	Mileage at Service:
Service Provider:	Cost:

Scope of Work: _____
_____
_____

Review/Notes: _____
_____
_____

Service Record Sheet

Service Date:	Mileage at Service:
Service Provider:	Cost:

Scope of Work: _____
_____
_____

Review/Notes: _____
_____
_____

Service Date:	Mileage at Service:
Service Provider:	Cost:

Scope of Work: _____
_____
_____

Review/Notes: _____
_____
_____

Service Date:	Mileage at Service:
Service Provider:	Cost:

Scope of Work: _____
_____
_____

Review/Notes: _____
_____
_____

Service Record Sheet

Service Date:	Mileage at Service:
Service Provider:	Cost:

Scope of Work: _____

_____

_____

Review/Notes: _____

_____

_____

Service Date:	Mileage at Service:
Service Provider:	Cost:

Scope of Work: _____

_____

_____

Review/Notes: _____

_____

_____

Service Date:	Mileage at Service:
Service Provider:	Cost:

Scope of Work: _____

_____

_____

Review/Notes: _____

_____

_____

Service Record Sheet

Service Date:	Mileage at Service:
Service Provider:	Cost:

Scope of Work: _____
_____
_____

Review/Notes: _____
_____
_____

Service Date:	Mileage at Service:
Service Provider:	Cost:

Scope of Work: _____
_____
_____

Review/Notes: _____
_____
_____

Service Date:	Mileage at Service:
Service Provider:	Cost:

Scope of Work: _____
_____
_____

Review/Notes: _____
_____
_____

Service Record Sheet

Service Date:	Mileage at Service:
Service Provider:	Cost:

Scope of Work: _____
_____
_____

Review/Notes: _____
_____
_____

Service Date:	Mileage at Service:
Service Provider:	Cost:

Scope of Work: _____
_____
_____

Revlew/Notes: _____
_____
_____

Service Date:	Mileage at Service:
Service Provider:	Cost:

Scope of Work: _____
_____
_____

Review/Notes: _____
_____
_____

Service Record Sheet

Service Date:	Mileage at Service:
Service Provider:	Cost:

Scope of Work: _____
_____
_____

Review/Notes: _____
_____
_____

Service Date:	Mileage at Service:
Service Provider:	Cost:

Scope of Work: _____
_____
_____

Review/Notes: _____
_____
_____

Service Date:	Mileage at Service:
Service Provider:	Cost:

Scope of Work: _____
_____
_____

Review/Notes: _____
_____
_____

Service Record Sheet

Service Date:	Mileage at Service:
Service Provider:	Cost:

Scope of Work: _____
_____
_____

Review/Notes: _____
_____
_____

Service Date:	Mileage at Service:
Service Provider:	Cost:

Scope of Work: _____
_____
_____

Review/Notes: _____
_____
_____

Service Date:	Mileage at Service:
Service Provider:	Cost:

Scope of Work: _____
_____
_____

Review/Notes: _____
_____
_____

Service Record Sheet

Service Date:	Mileage at Service:
Service Provider:	Cost:

Scope of Work: _____

_____

_____

Review/Notes: _____

_____

_____

Service Date:	Mileage at Service:
Service Provider:	Cost:

Scope of Work: _____

_____

_____

Review/Notes: _____

_____

_____

Service Date:	Mileage at Service:
Service Provider:	Cost:

Scope of Work: _____

_____

_____

Review/Notes: _____

_____

_____

Service Record Sheet

Service Date:	Mileage at Service:
Service Provider:	Cost:

Scope of Work: _____
_____
_____

Review/Notes: _____
_____
_____

Service Date:	Mileage at Service:
Service Provider:	Cost:

Scope of Work: _____
_____
_____

Review/Notes: _____
_____
_____

Service Date:	Mileage at Service:
Service Provider:	Cost:

Scope of Work: _____
_____
_____

Review/Notes: _____
_____
_____

Service Record Sheet

Service Date:	Mileage at Service:
Service Provider:	Cost:

Scope of Work: _____
_____
_____

Review/Notes: _____
_____
_____

Service Date:	Mileage at Service:
Service Provider:	Cost:

Scope of Work: _____
_____
_____

Review/Notes: _____
_____
_____

Service Date:	Mileage at Service:
Service Provider:	Cost:

Scope of Work: _____
_____
_____

Review/Notes: _____
_____
_____

Service Record Sheet

Service Date:	Mileage at Service:
Service Provider:	Cost:

Scope of Work: _____
_____
_____
_____

Review/Notes: _____
_____
_____

Service Date:	Mileage at Service:
Service Provider:	Cost:

Scope of Work: _____
_____
_____
_____

Review/Notes: _____
_____
_____

Service Date:	Mileage at Service:
Service Provider:	Cost:

Scope of Work: _____
_____
_____
_____

Review/Notes: _____
_____
_____

Service Record Sheet

Service Date:	Mileage at Service:
Service Provider:	Cost:

Scope of Work: _____

_____

_____

Review/Notes: _____

_____

_____

Service Date:	Mileage at Service:
Service Provider:	Cost:

Scope of Work: _____

_____

_____

Review/Notes: _____

_____

_____

Service Date:	Mileage at Service:
Service Provider:	Cost:

Scope of Work: _____

_____

_____

Review/Notes: _____

_____

_____

Service Record Sheet

Service Date:	Mileage at Service:
Service Provider:	Cost:

Scope of Work: _____
_____
_____

Review/Notes: _____
_____
_____

Service Date:	Mileage at Service:
Service Provider:	Cost:

Scope of Work: _____
_____
_____

Review/Notes: _____
_____
_____

Service Date:	Mileage at Service:
Service Provider:	Cost:

Scope of Work: _____
_____
_____

Review/Notes: _____
_____
_____

Service Record Sheet

Service Date:	Mileage at Service:
Service Provider:	Cost:

Scope of Work: _____
_____
_____

Review/Notes: _____
_____
_____

Service Date:	Mileage at Service:
Service Provider:	Cost:

Scope of Work: _____
_____
_____

Review/Notes: _____
_____
_____

Service Date:	Mileage at Service:
Service Provider:	Cost:

Scope of Work: _____
_____
_____

Review/Notes: _____
_____
_____

Service Record Sheet

Service Date:	Mileage at Service:
Service Provider:	Cost:

Scope of Work: _____

_____

_____

Review/Notes: _____

_____

_____

Service Date:	Mileage at Service:
Service Provider:	Cost:

Scope of Work: _____

_____

_____

Review/Notes: _____

_____

_____

Service Date:	Mileage at Service:
Service Provider:	Cost:

Scope of Work: _____

_____

_____

Review/Notes: _____

_____

_____

Service Record Sheet

Service Date:	Mileage at Service:
Service Provider:	Cost:

Scope of Work: _____

_____

_____

Review/Notes: _____

_____

_____

Service Date:	Mileage at Service:
Service Provider:	Cost:

Scope of Work: _____

_____

_____

Review/Notes: _____

_____

_____

Service Date:	Mileage at Service:
Service Provider:	Cost:

Scope of Work: _____

_____

_____

Review/Notes: _____

_____

_____

Service Record Sheet

Service Date:	Mileage at Service:
Service Provider:	Cost:

Scope of Work: _____
_____
_____

Review/Notes: _____
_____
_____

Service Date:	Mileage at Service:
Service Provider:	Cost:

Scope of Work: _____
_____
_____

Review/Notes: _____
_____
_____

Service Date:	Mileage at Service:
Service Provider:	Cost:

Scope of Work:
_____
_____

Review/Notes: _____
_____
_____

Service Record Sheet

Service Date:	Mileage at Service:
Service Provider:	Cost:

Scope of Work: _____

_____

_____

Review/Notes: _____

_____

_____

Service Date:	Mileage at Service:
Service Provider:	Cost:

Scope of Work: _____

_____

_____

Review/Notes: _____

_____

_____

Service Date:	Mileage at Service:
Service Provider:	Cost:

Scope of Work: _____

_____

_____

Review/Notes: _____

_____

_____

Service Record Sheet

Service Date:	Mileage at Service:
Service Provider:	Cost:

Scope of Work: _____
_____
_____

Review/Notes: _____
_____
_____

Service Date:	Mileage at Service:
Service Provider:	Cost:

Scope of Work: _____
_____
_____

Review/Notes: _____
_____
_____

Service Date:	Mileage at Service:
Service Provider:	Cost:

Scope of Work: _____
_____
_____

Review/Notes: _____
_____
_____

Service Record Sheet

Service Date:	Mileage at Service:
Service Provider:	Cost:

Scope of Work: _____

_____

_____

Review/Notes: _____

_____

_____

Service Date:	Mileage at Service:
Service Provider:	Cost:

Scope of Work: _____

_____

_____

Review/Notes: _____

_____

_____

Service Date:	Mileage at Service:
Service Provider:	Cost:

Scope of Work: _____

_____

_____

Review/Notes: _____

_____

_____

Service Record Sheet

Service Date:	Mileage at Service:
Service Provider:	Cost:

Scope of Work: _____
_____
_____

Review/Notes: _____
_____
_____

Service Date:	Mileage at Service:
Service Provider:	Cost:

Scope of Work: _____
_____
_____

Review/Notes: _____
_____
_____

Service Date:	Mileage at Service:
Service Provider:	Cost:

Scope of Work: _____
_____
_____

Review/Notes: _____
_____
_____

Service Record Sheet

Service Date:	Mileage at Service:
Service Provider:	Cost:

Scope of Work: _____
_____
_____

Review/Notes: _____
_____
_____

Service Date:	Mileage at Service:
Service Provider:	Cost:

Scope of Work: _____
_____
_____

Review/Notes: _____
_____
_____

Service Date:	Mileage at Service:
Service Provider:	Cost:

Scope of Work: _____
_____
_____

Review/Notes: _____
_____
_____

Service Record Sheet

Service Date:	Mileage at Service:
Service Provider:	Cost:

Scope of Work: _____
_____
_____

Review/Notes: _____
_____
_____

Service Date:	Mileage at Service:
Service Provider:	Cost:

Scope of Work: _____
_____
_____

Review/Notes: _____
_____
_____

Service Date:	Mileage at Service:
Service Provider:	Cost:

Scope of Work: _____
_____
_____

Review/Notes: _____
_____
_____

Service Record Sheet

Service Date:	Mileage at Service:
Service Provider:	Cost:

Scope of Work: _____

_____

_____

Review/Notes: _____

_____

_____

Service Date:	Mileage at Service:
Service Provider:	Cost:

Scope of Work: _____

_____

_____

Review/Notes: _____

_____

_____

Service Date:	Mileage at Service:
Service Provider:	Cost:

Scope of Work: _____

_____

_____

Review/Notes: _____

_____

_____

Service Record Sheet

Service Date:	Mileage at Service:
Service Provider:	Cost:

Scope of Work: _____
_____
_____

Review/Notes: _____
_____
_____

Service Date:	Mileage at Service:
Service Provider:	Cost:

Scope of Work: _____
_____
_____

Review/Notes: _____
_____
_____

Service Date:	Mileage at Service:
Service Provider:	Cost:

Scope of Work: _____
_____
_____

Review/Notes: _____
_____
_____

Service Record Sheet

Service Date:	Mileage at Service:
Service Provider:	Cost:

Scope of Work: _____
_____
_____

Review/Notes: _____
_____
_____

Service Date:	Mileage at Service:
Service Provider:	Cost:

Scope of Work: _____
_____
_____

Review/Notes: _____
_____
_____

Service Date:	Mileage at Service:
Service Provider:	Cost:

Scope of Work: _____
_____
_____

Review/Notes: _____
_____
_____

Service Record Sheet

Service Date:	Mileage at Service:
Service Provider:	Cost:

Scope of Work: _____
_____
_____

Review/Notes: _____
_____
_____

Service Date:	Mileage at Service:
Service Provider:	Cost:

Scope of Work: _____
_____
_____

Review/Notes: _____
_____
_____

Service Date:	Mileage at Service:
Service Provider:	Cost:

Scope of Work: _____
_____
_____

Review/Notes: _____
_____
_____

Service Record Sheet

Service Date:	Mileage at Service:
Service Provider:	Cost:

Scope of Work: _____
_____
_____

Review/Notes: _____
_____
_____

Service Date:	Mileage at Service:
Service Provider:	Cost:

Scope of Work: _____
_____
_____

Review/Notes: _____
_____
_____

Service Date:	Mileage at Service:
Service Provider:	Cost:

Scope of Work: _____
_____
_____

Review/Notes: _____
_____
_____

Service Record Sheet

Service Date:	Mileage at Service:
Service Provider:	Cost:

Scope of Work: _____
_____
_____

Review/Notes: _____
_____
_____

Service Date:	Mileage at Service:
Service Provider:	Cost:

Scope of Work: _____
_____
_____

Review/Notes: _____
_____
_____

Service Date:	Mileage at Service:
Service Provider:	Cost:

Scope of Work: _____
_____
_____

Review/Notes: _____
_____
_____

Service Record Sheet

Service Date:	Mileage at Service:
Service Provider:	Cost:

Scope of Work: _____

_____

_____

Review/Notes: _____

_____

_____

Service Date:	Mileage at Service:
Service Provider:	Cost:

Scope of Work: _____

_____

_____

Review/Notes: _____

_____

_____

Service Date:	Mileage at Service:
Service Provider:	Cost:

Scope of Work: _____

_____

_____

Review/Notes: _____

_____

_____

Service Record Sheet

Service Date:	Mileage at Service:
Service Provider:	Cost:

Scope of Work: _____

_____

_____

Review/Notes: _____

_____

_____

Service Date:	Mileage at Service:
Service Provider:	Cost:

Scope of Work: _____

_____

_____

Review/Notes: _____

_____

_____

Service Date:	Mileage at Service:
Service Provider:	Cost:

Scope of Work: _____

_____

_____

Review/Notes: _____

_____

_____

Service Record Sheet

Service Date:	Mileage at Service:
Service Provider:	Cost:

Scope of Work: _____
_____
_____

Review/Notes: _____
_____
_____

Service Date:	Mileage at Service:
Service Provider:	Cost:

Scope of Work: _____
_____
_____

Review/Notes: _____
_____
_____

Service Date:	Mileage at Service:
Service Provider:	Cost:

Scope of Work: _____
_____
_____

Review/Notes: _____
_____
_____

Service Record Sheet

Service Date:	Mileage at Service:
Service Provider:	Cost:

Scope of Work: _____
_____
_____

Review/Notes: _____
_____
_____

Service Date:	Mileage at Service:
Service Provider:	Cost:

Scope of Work: _____
_____
_____

Review/Notes: _____
_____
_____

Service Date:	Mileage at Service:
Service Provider:	Cost:

Scope of Work: _____
_____
_____

Review/Notes: _____
_____
_____

Service Record Sheet

Service Date:	Mileage at Service:
Service Provider:	Cost:

Scope of Work: _____
_____
_____

Review/Notes: _____
_____
_____

Service Date:	Mileage at Service:
Service Provider:	Cost:

Scope of Work: _____
_____
_____

Review/Notes: _____
_____
_____

Service Date:	Mileage at Service:
Service Provider:	Cost:

Scope of Work: _____
_____
_____

Review/Notes: _____
_____
_____

Service Record Sheet

Service Date:	Mileage at Service:
Service Provider:	Cost:
Scope of Work: _____ _____ _____	
Review/Notes: _____ _____ _____	

Service Date:	Mileage at Service:
Service Provider:	Cost:
Scope of Work: _____ _____ _____	
Review/Notes: _____ _____ _____	

Service Date:	Mileage at Service:
Service Provider:	Cost:
Scope of Work: _____ _____ _____	
Review/Notes: _____ _____ _____	

Service Record Sheet

Service Date:	Mileage at Service:
Service Provider:	Cost:

Scope of Work: _____
_____
_____

Review/Notes: _____
_____
_____

Service Date:	Mileage at Service:
Service Provider:	Cost:

Scope of Work: _____
_____
_____

Review/Notes: _____
_____
_____

Service Date:	Mileage at Service:
Service Provider:	Cost:

Scope of Work: _____
_____
_____

Review/Notes: _____
_____
_____

Service Record Sheet

Service Date:	Mileage at Service:
Service Provider:	Cost:

Scope of Work: _____
_____
_____

Review/Notes: _____
_____
_____

Service Date:	Mileage at Service:
Service Provider:	Cost:

Scope of Work: _____
_____
_____

Review/Notes: _____
_____
_____

Service Date:	Mileage at Service:
Service Provider:	Cost:

Scope of Work: _____
_____
_____

Review/Notes: _____
_____
_____

Service Record Sheet

Service Date:	Mileage at Service:
Service Provider:	Cost:

Scope of Work: _____
_____
_____

Review/Notes: _____
_____
_____

Service Date:	Mileage at Service:
Service Provider:	Cost:

Scope of Work: _____
_____
_____

Review/Notes: _____
_____
_____

Service Date:	Mileage at Service:
Service Provider:	Cost:

Scope of Work: _____
_____
_____

Review/Notes: _____
_____
_____

Service Record Sheet

Service Date:	Mileage at Service:
Service Provider:	Cost:

Scope of Work: _____
_____
_____

Review/Notes: _____
_____
_____

Service Date:	Mileage at Service:
Service Provider:	Cost:

Scope of Work: _____
_____
_____

Review/Notes: _____
_____
_____

Service Date:	Mileage at Service:
Service Provider:	Cost:

Scope of Work: _____
_____
_____

Review/Notes: _____
_____
_____

Service Record Sheet

Service Date:	Mileage at Service:
Service Provider:	Cost:

Scope of Work: _____
_____
_____

Review/Notes: _____
_____
_____

Service Date:	Mileage at Service:
Service Provider:	Cost:

Scope of Work: _____
_____
_____

Review/Notes: _____
_____
_____

Service Date:	Mileage at Service:
Service Provider:	Cost:

Scope of Work: _____
_____
_____

Review/Notes: _____
_____
_____

Service Record Sheet

Service Date:	Mileage at Service:
Service Provider:	Cost:

Scope of Work: _____
_____
_____

Review/Notes: _____
_____
_____

Service Date:	Mileage at Service:
Service Provider:	Cost:

Scope of Work: _____
_____
_____

Review/Notes: _____
_____
_____

Service Date:	Mileage at Service:
Service Provider:	Cost:

Scope of Work: _____
_____
_____

Review/Notes: _____
_____
_____

Service Record Sheet

Service Date:	Mileage at Service:
Service Provider:	Cost:

Scope of Work: _____
_____
_____

Review/Notes: _____
_____
_____

Service Date:	Mileage at Service:
Service Provider:	Cost:

Scope of Work: _____
_____
_____

Review/Notes: _____
_____
_____

Service Date:	Mileage at Service:
Service Provider:	Cost:

Scope of Work: _____
_____
_____

Review/Notes: _____
_____
_____

Service Record Sheet

Service Date:	Mileage at Service:
Service Provider:	Cost:

Scope of Work: _____
_____
_____

Review/Notes: _____
_____
_____

Service Date:	Mileage at Service:
Service Provider:	Cost:

Scope of Work: _____
_____
_____

Review/Notes: _____
_____
_____

Service Date:	Mileage at Service:
Service Provider:	Cost:

Scope of Work: _____
_____
_____

Review/Notes: _____
_____
_____

Service Record Sheet

Service Date:	Mileage at Service:
Service Provider:	Cost:

Scope of Work: _____
_____
_____

Review/Notes: _____
_____
_____

Service Date:	Mileage at Service:
Service Provider:	Cost:

Scope of Work: _____
_____
_____

Review/Notes: _____
_____
_____

Service Date:	Mileage at Service:
Service Provider:	Cost:

Scope of Work: _____
_____
_____

Review/Notes: _____
_____
_____

Service Record Sheet

Service Date:	Mileage at Service:
Service Provider:	Cost:

Scope of Work: _____
_____
_____

Review/Notes: _____
_____
_____

Service Date:	Mileage at Service:
Service Provider:	Cost:

Scope of Work: _____
_____
_____

Review/Notes: _____
_____
_____

Service Date:	Mileage at Service:
Service Provider:	Cost:

Scope of Work: _____
_____
_____

Review/Notes: _____
_____
_____

Service Record Sheet

Service Date:	Mileage at Service:
Service Provider:	Cost:

Scope of Work: _____

_____

_____

Review/Notes: _____

_____

_____

Service Date:	Mileage at Service:
Service Provider:	Cost:

Scope of Work: _____

_____

_____

Review/Notes: _____

_____

_____

Service Date:	Mileage at Service:
Service Provider:	Cost:

Scope of Work: _____

_____

_____

Review/Notes: _____

_____

_____

Service Record Sheet

Service Date:	Mileage at Service:
Service Provider:	Cost:

Scope of Work: _____
_____
_____

Review/Notes: _____
_____
_____

Service Date:	Mileage at Service:
Service Provider:	Cost:

Scope of Work: _____
_____
_____

Review/Notes: _____
_____
_____

Service Date:	Mileage at Service:
Service Provider:	Cost:

Scope of Work: _____
_____
_____

Review/Notes: _____
_____
_____

Service Record Sheet

Service Date:	Mileage at Service:
Service Provider:	Cost:

Scope of Work: _____

_____

_____

Review/Notes: _____

_____

_____

Service Date:	Mileage at Service:
Service Provider:	Cost:

Scope of Work: _____

_____

_____

Review/Notes: _____

_____

_____

Service Date:	Mileage at Service:
Service Provider:	Cost:

Scope of Work: _____

_____

_____

Review/Notes: _____

_____

_____

Service Record Sheet

Service Date:	Mileage at Service:
Service Provider:	Cost:

Scope of Work: _____
_____
_____

Review/Notes: _____
_____
_____

Service Date:	Mileage at Service:
Service Provider:	Cost:

Scope of Work: _____
_____
_____

Review/Notes: _____
_____
_____

Service Date:	Mileage at Service:
Service Provider:	Cost:

Scope of Work: _____
_____
_____

Review/Notes: _____
_____
_____

Service Record Sheet

Service Date:	Mileage at Service:
Service Provider:	Cost:

Scope of Work: _____
_____
_____

Review/Notes: _____
_____
_____

Service Date:	Mileage at Service:
Service Provider:	Cost:

Scope of Work: _____
_____
_____

Review/Notes: _____
_____
_____

Service Date:	Mileage at Service:
Service Provider:	Cost:

Scope of Work: _____
_____
_____

Review/Notes: _____
_____
_____

Service Record Sheet

Service Date:	Mileage at Service:
Service Provider:	Cost:

Scope of Work: _____
_____
_____

Review/Notes: _____
_____
_____

Service Date:	Mileage at Service:
Service Provider:	Cost:

Scope of Work: _____
_____
_____

Review/Notes: _____
_____
_____

Service Date:	Mileage at Service:
Service Provider:	Cost:

Scope of Work: _____
_____
_____

Review/Notes: _____
_____
_____

Service Record Sheet

Service Date:	Mileage at Service:
Service Provider:	Cost:

Scope of Work: _____
_____
_____

Review/Notes: _____
_____
_____

Service Date:	Mileage at Service:
Service Provider:	Cost:

Scope of Work: _____
_____
_____

Review/Notes: _____
_____
_____

Service Date:	Mileage at Service:
Service Provider:	Cost:

Scope of Work: _____
_____
_____

Review/Notes: _____
_____
_____

Service Record Sheet

Service Date:	Mileage at Service:
Service Provider:	Cost:

Scope of Work: _____

_____

_____

Review/Notes: _____

_____

_____

Service Date:	Mileage at Service:
Service Provider:	Cost:

Scope of Work: _____

_____

_____

Review/Notes: _____

_____

_____

Service Date:	Mileage at Service:
Service Provider:	Cost:

Scope of Work: _____

_____

_____

Review/Notes: _____

_____

_____

Service Record Sheet

Service Date:	Mileage at Service:
Service Provider:	Cost:

Scope of Work: _____
_____
_____

Review/Notes: _____
_____
_____

Service Date:	Mileage at Service:
Service Provider:	Cost:

Scope of Work: _____
_____
_____

Review/Notes: _____
_____
_____

Service Date:	Mileage at Service:
Service Provider:	Cost:

Scope of Work: _____
_____
_____

Review/Notes: _____
_____
_____

Service Record Sheet

Service Date:	Mileage at Service:
Service Provider:	Cost:

Scope of Work: _____
_____
_____

Review/Notes: _____
_____
_____

Service Date:	Mileage at Service:
Service Provider:	Cost:

Scope of Work: _____
_____
_____

Review/Notes: _____
_____
_____

Service Date:	Mileage at Service:
Service Provider:	Cost:

Scope of Work: _____
_____
_____

Review/Notes: _____
_____
_____

Service Record Sheet

Service Date:	Mileage at Service:
Service Provider:	Cost:

Scope of Work: _____
_____
_____

Review/Notes: _____
_____
_____

Service Date:	Mileage at Service:
Service Provider:	Cost:

Scope of Work: _____
_____
_____

Review/Notes: _____
_____
_____

Service Date:	Mileage at Service:
Service Provider:	Cost:

Scope of Work: _____
_____
_____

Review/Notes: _____
_____
_____

Service Record Sheet

Service Date:	Mileage at Service:
Service Provider:	Cost:

Scope of Work: _____

_____

_____

Review/Notes: _____

_____

_____

Service Date:	Mileage at Service:
Service Provider:	Cost:

Scope of Work: _____

_____

_____

Review/Notes: _____

_____

_____

Service Date:	Mileage at Service:
Service Provider:	Cost:

Scope of Work: _____

_____

_____

Review/Notes: _____

_____

_____

Service Record Sheet

Service Date:	Mileage at Service:
Service Provider:	Cost:

Scope of Work: _____
_____
_____

Review/Notes: _____
_____
_____

Service Date:	Mileage at Service:
Service Provider:	Cost:

Scope of Work: _____
_____
_____

Review/Notes: _____
_____
_____

Service Date:	Mileage at Service:
Service Provider:	Cost:

Scope of Work: _____
_____
_____

Review/Notes: _____
_____
_____

Service Record Sheet

Service Date:	Mileage at Service:
Service Provider:	Cost:

Scope of Work: _____
_____
_____

Review/Notes: _____
_____
_____

Service Date:	Mileage at Service:
Service Provider:	Cost:

Scope of Work: _____
_____
_____

Review/Notes: _____
_____
_____

Service Date:	Mileage at Service:
Service Provider:	Cost:

Scope of Work: _____
_____
_____

Review/Notes: _____
_____
_____

Service Record Sheet

Service Date:	Mileage at Service:
Service Provider:	Cost:

Scope of Work: _____
_____
_____

Review/Notes: _____
_____
_____

Service Date:	Mileage at Service:
Service Provider:	Cost:

Scope of Work: _____
_____
_____

Review/Notes: _____
_____
_____

Service Date:	Mileage at Service:
Service Provider:	Cost:

Scope of Work: _____
_____
_____

Review/Notes: _____
_____
_____

Service Record Sheet

Service Date:	Mileage at Service:
Service Provider:	Cost:

Scope of Work: _____
_____
_____

Review/Notes: _____
_____
_____

Service Date:	Mileage at Service:
Service Provider:	Cost:

Scope of Work: _____
_____
_____

Review/Notes: _____
_____
_____

Service Date:	Mileage at Service:
Service Provider:	Cost:

Scope of Work: _____
_____
_____

Review/Notes: _____
_____
_____

Service Record Sheet

Service Date:	Mileage at Service:
Service Provider:	Cost:

Scope of Work: _____
_____
_____

Review/Notes: _____
_____
_____

Service Date:	Mileage at Service:
Service Provider:	Cost:

Scope of Work: _____
_____
_____

Review/Notes: _____
_____
_____

Service Date:	Mileage at Service:
Service Provider:	Cost:

Scope of Work: _____
_____
_____

Review/Notes: _____
_____
_____

Service Record Sheet

Service Date:	Mileage at Service:
Service Provider:	Cost:

Scope of Work: _____
_____
_____

Review/Notes: _____
_____
_____

Service Date:	Mileage at Service:
Service Provider:	Cost:

Scope of Work: _____
_____
_____

Review/Notes: _____
_____
_____

Service Date:	Mileage at Service:
Service Provider:	Cost:

Scope of Work: _____
_____
_____

Review/Notes: _____
_____
_____